A Locomobile runabout, with four proper seats, mounted on an extended wheelbase. This vehicle dates from 1902 and was kept in India. A hood was not necessary as it was probably never driven in the rain, which falls only during the monsoon in India. The car is being driven by Major the Nawab Afsur Dowla of Bahadur, accompanied by his two sons and Colonel Marshall.

STEAM CARS

Richard J. Evans

Shire Publications Ltd

CONTENTS

Set in 9 point Times roman and printed in Great Britain by C. I. Thomas & Sons (Haverfordwest) Ltd, Merlins Bridge, Haverfordwest, Dyfed.

British Library Cataloguing in Publication Data available.

Editorial Consultant: Michael E. Ware, Curator of the National Motor Museum, Beaulieu.

ACKNOWLEDGEMENTS

The illustrations, except for those on the front cover and pages 29 and 30, are from the National Motor Museum Photographic Library and are reproduced by kind permission of the National Motor Museum, Beaulieu. The photographs on pages 29 and 30 are acknowledged to General Motors and the cover photograph to the Manx Motor Museum.

COVER: *A Stanley steam car of 1904 in steam. This is a model CX, rated at 8 horsepower, giving a maximum speed of about 45 mph (72 km/h), consuming unleaded petrol at about 5 miles per gallon (1.77 km/litre) and water at 1 mile per gallon (0.35 km/litre). The car's tank holds 20 gallons (91 litres) of water and so refilling stops, at a horse trough or stream, would be needed every 20 miles (32 km). The acceleration is approximately equal to that of a 50 horsepower petrol car of the same period.*

BELOW: *This diagram shows every essential part of the Stanley steam car except the axle, body and steering gear assemblies. It includes boiler, burner and engine, and fuel, steam and water systems complete with every valve and pipe on the car. It demonstrates the simplicity of the Stanley, compared with internal explosive cars.*

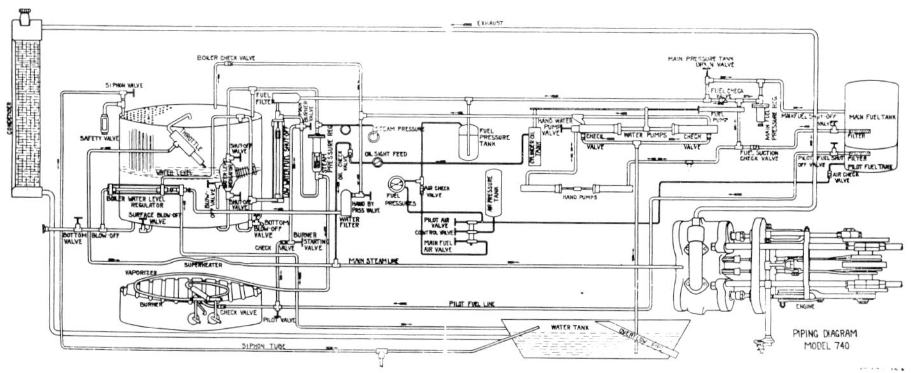

This historic photograph depicts the twins F. E. and F. O. Stanley, in one of their first cars during 1897. This was the design which they sold to Locomobile for 250,000 dollars and a few years later bought back for 20,000 dollars. This early example has few controls and little equipment, the object at this stage being to prove their basic design. Thus there are no mudguards or hood, and few instruments. The engine is vertically placed under the seat, with the boiler close behind it.

INTRODUCTION

In their heyday during the early years of the twentieth century steam cars were as numerous, if not more so, than petrol cars, especially in the United States. Once ease of operation of the internal combustion engine had been achieved, steam and the equally numerous electric cars fell out of fashion; although they have continued to be made to the present day, albeit in small numbers, nearly all modern productions have been experimental.

Without steam power to drive machinery and provide reliable transport by water and land, industrial development would have been much slower, and it is more than probable that, even by the twenty-first century, the necessary tooling and power could not have been produced to give the world private transport as we know it today. Before steam was developed, industrial power was based on water and wind, both too variable by nature to give sufficiently reliable power for efficient industrial production.

The idea of making self-propelled private carriages developed significantly after about 1880, and internal combustion was soon to rival steam, although the latter had a head start, being already well developed for heavy transport by sea, canal and rail, but with only a limited application on the road in the form of the traction engine.

However, the requirements of these modes of transport were different from that of a private car. Water and rail transport usually consisted of moving a large load at a relatively constant speed, with a minimum of starting and stopping, and with no gradients on water, and only very easy ones by rail. For this purpose coal was an ideal fuel to provide a steady supply of steam. But a private carriage needed a source of heat that could be quickly varied to allow for the different demands on steam that frequent starting

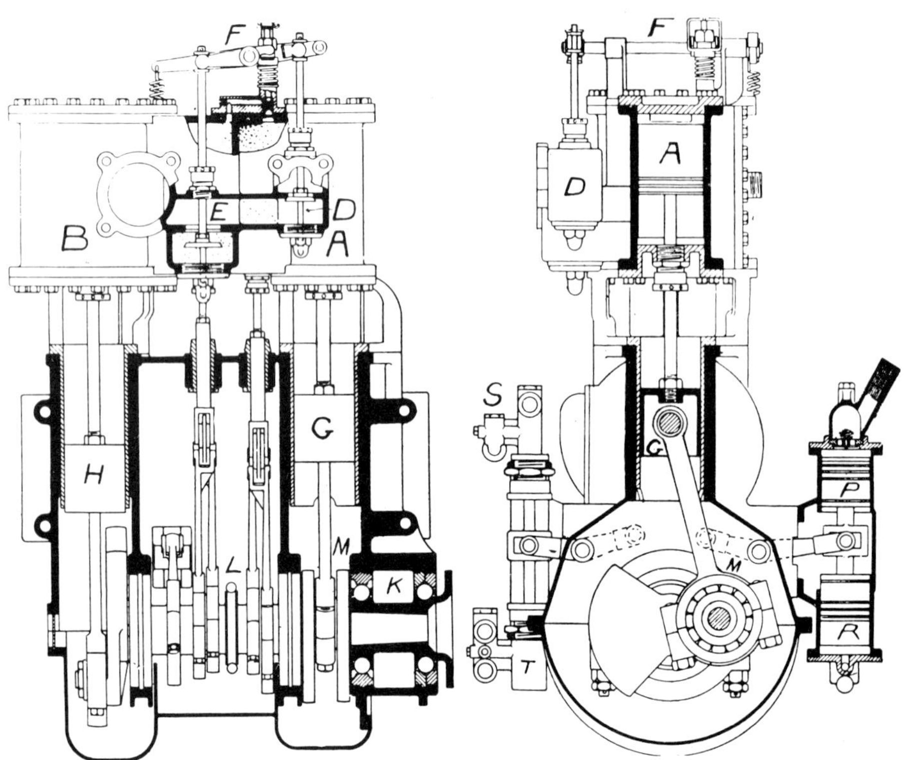

A typical White compound engine of about 1907. A is the high-pressure cylinder, B the low-pressure cylinder; D and E are the respective poppet valves, operated by the rocking lever F. G and H are the cross-heads which support the outer ends of the piston rods, to ensure that they run parallel to the pistons and that a seal can thus be maintained around them. These rods then drive the crankshaft through the medium of connecting rods and big ends (M). L is the eccentric drive for the valves. P, R, S and T are the auxiliary pumps for fuel, water and oil.

and stopping and changes of speed and gradient required. Petrol seemed to be the best choice.

It has been said that the petrol companies killed the steam car but this is not so. Because a steam car burns fuel outside the engine it is far more inefficient than the 'internal' combustion engine, thus the consumption of fuel (petrol) by a steam car per mile, per mile per hour or per pound weight is much greater than by the petrol car, even excluding the extra fuel burnt when raising steam from cold in many designs. The oil companies had no wish to kill the steamer. Its demise was brought about by fear, com-plication and cost, none of which were worthwhile once the internal combustion engine had become reliable and easy to operate, the electric self-starter being the decisive factor.

CONTROL OF STEAM

The basic principle of steam power is simply that water when heated turns into vapour which can be held in a compress-ed state and released as required to provide power. Apart from one or two modern experiments, this power in the case of steam cars has always been applied through the medium of a sliding piston in a cylinder, the reciprocal motion

A Doble engine. Various modifications were made to Abner Doble's engine, despite the small number made. This is a cross-section of a typical model, a twin-cylinder single-expansion double-acting engine. It can be seen that the connecting-rod big ends have roller bearings, which are extensively used throughout the design. The spur gear on the crankshaft meshes directly with another spur gear surrounding the final drive unit, making a compact unit, albeit at the expense of unsprung weight.

thus produced being transferred to rotation at the wheels by suitable mechanical gearing.

The principle is extremely simple, but the complication of control has always been the bugbear, there being two major problems, consumption of water and getting the right amount of heat into the water at the right time. The first was the easier to solve, by condensing the exhaust steam and returning the resultant water to the supply tank, leaving only the difficulty, admittedly a significant one, of removing the cylinder lubricating oil from the exhaust first.

Getting the right amount of heat at the appropriate time was, and still is, the most serious problem; in the end the complications of trying to do this automatically were so great that the steamer became much more complex than the internal combustion engine.

A few private vehicles had coal-fired burners, but these were always very difficult to control and liquid fuel made the advent of the light steam buggy feasible. Vast numbers were made in the early years of the twentieth century, mostly based on the two-cylinder simple engine, with a few adventurous people trying variations on the compound engine.

ENGINES

The piston sliding up and down the cylinder was normally attached to a connecting rod, the other end of which drove a crankshaft, which in turn transmitted power to the wheels.

The simplest variation was a single-cylinder, single-acting design, in which the steam pushes the piston one way only, momentum bringing it back the other way. This needed a very heavy flywheel to work and was hardly ever used for other than stationary engines, as it was seldom self-starting. A twin cylinder single-acting engine will often self-start, but far better was a twin-cylinder double-acting engine, that is with the steam pushing the piston both ways, or a three-cylinder design. An engine with more than three cylinders will always self-start.

It is a more economical design to use double-acting engines, but the problem then exists of maintaining a steam-tight seal around the connecting rod, during one part of the cycle.

The other type of engine often used, though not so much in the early days, is the compound. In this design the steam, having first passed into the smaller-diameter cylinder or cylinders, exhausts to larger cylinders and finally to atmosphere or the condenser, whereas in a simple engine not all the power of the steam is used up in the first cylinder and much is wasted. This can be partially recovered by using it in a larger-diameter cylinder, in which volume makes up for a reduced pressure. In practice it is usual to make these high and low pressure cylinders in one unit, with all pistons acting on the same crankshaft.

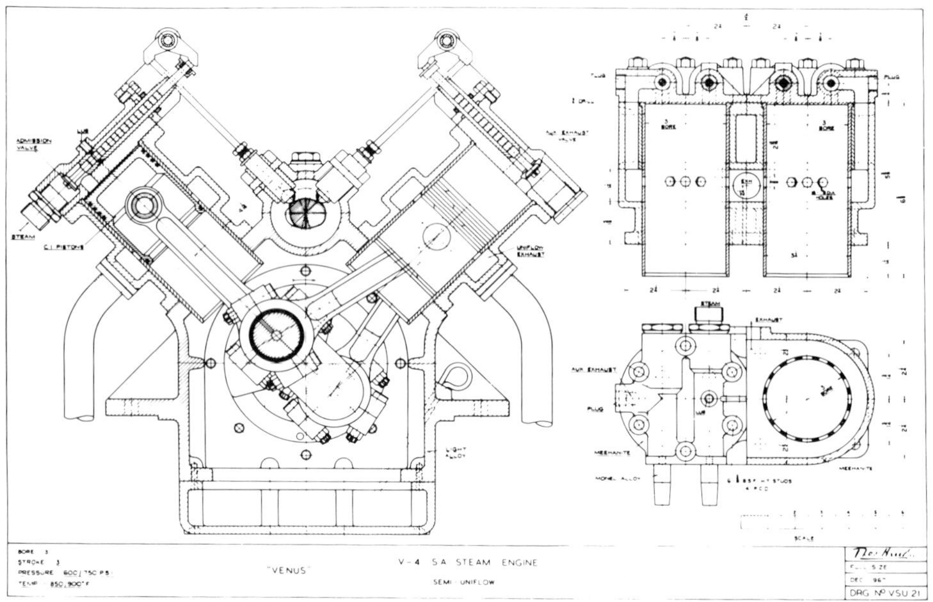

This is a Thomas Hindle design of 1967 for a V4 steam engine of semi-uniflow type. It used steam at a pressure of 600 to 750 pounds per square inch (42 to 53 kg/sq cm), with temperatures up to 900 Fahrenheit (482 Celsius). It had a 3 inch (76 mm) bore and a 3 inch (76 mm) stroke, thus being what is termed 'square'. Extensive use of Monel alloy was made in its construction, with ordinary alloy for sump and crankcase castings. An unusual type of horizontal poppet valve operated by a right-angle rocker system was employed. The engine was single-acting.

VALVE GEAR

There are many different types and designs of valve gear, but although valve gear is most important the various types are not. Usually the type used depends merely on the whim of the engine designer.

It is necessary to have valves to admit steam to each cylinder, or to each end of each cylinder as appropriate, in turn at the correct time — no more no less. Since steam engines can run in either direction and do not need to be left turning when the vehicle is at rest (unlike the internal combustion engine) it is an easy matter to provide reverse by admitting the steam at a different point in the engine's cycle. This, together with a function known as 'cut-off' is the main reason for the complication of valve gear. 'Cut-off' is the point in the piston's movement at which the steam admission is stopped or cut off, remaining piston movement being by steam expansion.

BOILERS

Anyone operating or close to a steam engine should be aware that they are not near a plaything and that steam power can be dangerous. Steam is an odd water vapour, which can be compressed and then released to provide power more or less continuously as it expands back to its uncompressed volume. The average steam car boiler contains a bucketful of steam and water, under the usual working pressures. If this were suddenly released to atmosphere, it would instantly expand to a volume of more than 1600 buckets — a lot of scalding vapour.

Water boils at 100 Celsius (212 Fahrenheit) at sea level, when not under pressure, but when confined in a boiler, and thus raised in pressure, its boiling point is much higher. Furthermore, before use the steam is often superheated by running it through a pipe immersed in the burner flames, thus increasing its temperature even more and producing

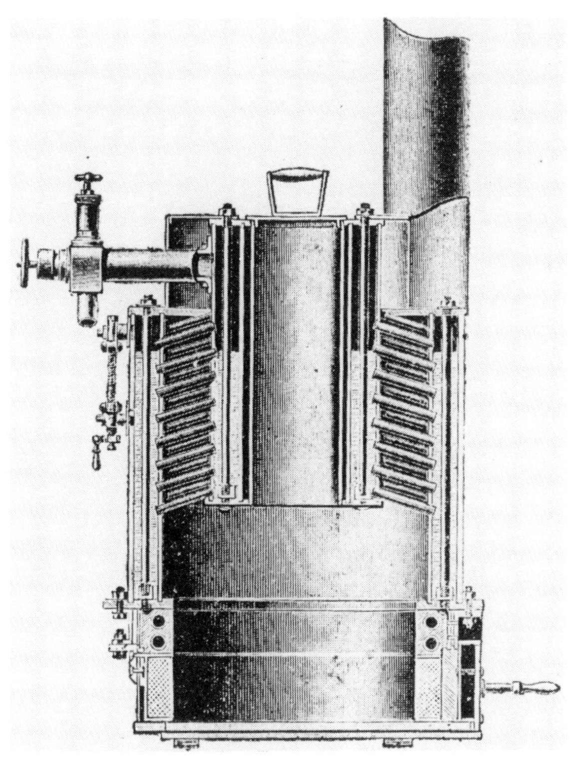

An early example of a car water-tube steam generator or boiler, designed by the De Dion company, most of the work being by De Dion's partner, Trepardoux. In this sectioned drawing, heat is provided by the burner at the bottom and rises past the small, almost horizontal tubes, heating the water they contain. This rises from the outer casing, as steam, which is collected in the central well, from where it is delivered to an engine, via the left-hand pipe.

A Turner-Meisse boiler, another type of flash boiler, comprising a long coil of steel tube made with numerous U turns to fit into a square casing. It is a continuous tube with water entering at the bottom, and steam emerging at the top. This example dates from 1904.

ABOVE: *A 1920 Stanley boiler, at the front of the car under a conventional bonnet, with a normal-shaped radiator as a condenser. The diameter of these boilers was about 2 feet (610 mm). The brass casting mounted vertically on the left of the scuttle is the steam automatic, which shuts off fuel when working pressure is reached.*

BELOW: *The White generator: an example of the water-tube or flash boiler used by White around 1908. Various arrangements of coiling a long length of steel tube were used, some with only two ends, one in and one out, others like this one with several circuits joined at each end. The complicated arrangement needed to feed water to the boiler and fuel to the burner beneath it can be seen. On the right is a valve for admitting auxiliary water to the boiler: the dial is a pyrometer, visible to the driver.*

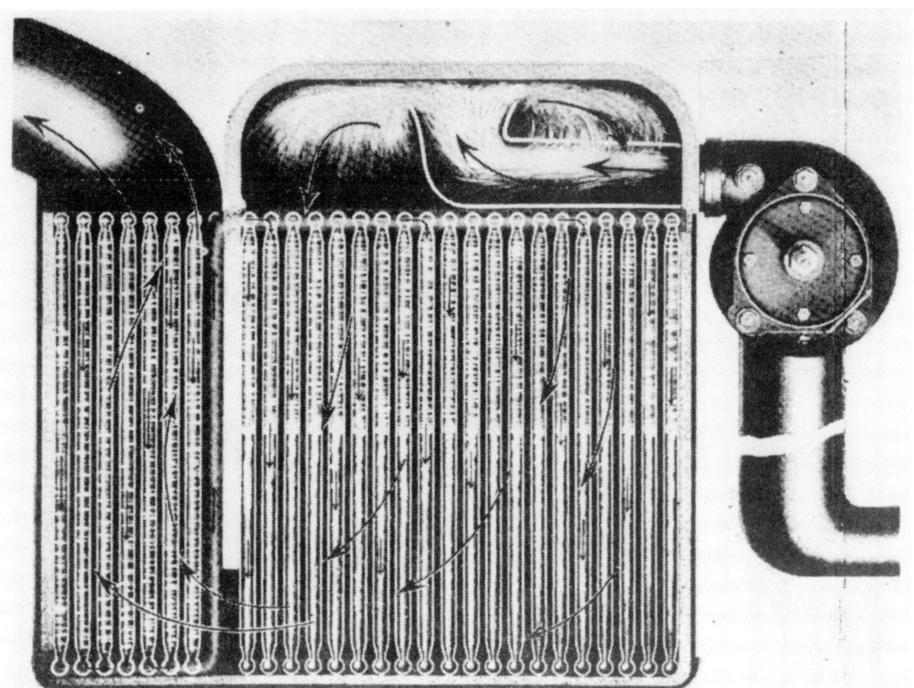

An early Doble boiler, consisting of a series of grids of vertical tubes, each being connected at the top and bottom. Water enters the bottom and steam comes out of the top. Each grid has about twenty tubes, about ¾ inch (19 mm) in diameter. The water tubes are surrounded by a lagged box to retain as much heat as possible. The burner fan on the left supplies forced fuel mixture for heating the water.

the so called 'dry' steam. This gives further expansion capabilities for use in the engine.

There are two main types of boiler, the fire-tube and the water-tube designs. In the fire-tube layout the heat from the burner passes up tubes to the chimney. The water surrounds these tubes and is thus heated, steam usually being collected in the top part of the boiler, the whole of which is surrounded and encased by a strong steel jacket.

The water-tube type is the reverse of the fire-tube layout: the water flows through tubes, which are surrounded by the fire. Their lower ends are connected to a water tank, and their upper ends lead to a tank which fills with steam. The 'flash boiler' is a variation of this design, in which cold or warm water enters at one end and passes through a long coil of tubing heated by the burner, so that steam emerges from the other end.

If a water-tube boiler bursts there is normally very little steam or hot water to escape and be dangerous. In the case of the fire-tube type, usually the fire tubes collapse inwards, allowing the water and steam to escape towards the centre, drowning the fire and losing much of its energy before it can reach anybody. It is rare for an outer casing to burst. Even in countries where boiler testing is not a legal requirement, it is sensible to check a boiler regularly by taking it up to twice working pressure with a cold-water test.

The flash boiler makes steam from cold more quickly, but the fire-tube type has the advantage that it has a reserve of steam, either for extra power, or for getting home if the burner goes wrong. In this case the boiler will tend to make more steam as its pressure drops, albeit with a lower energy content.

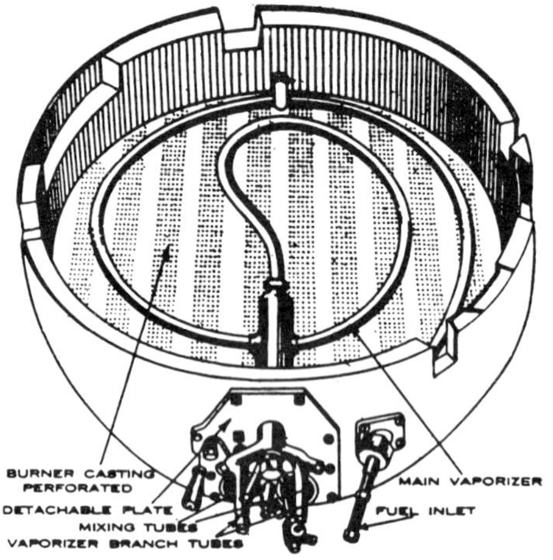

A vapourising type of burner used extensively during the early days of steam cars. Fuel entered the pipe on the right and ran around in the flame to become vapourised before being ejected at the main jets in the centre of the drawing. The heavy casting at the very centre was heated by the pilot light, to provide initial vapourisation. The burner-plate perforations could be either slots or holes. This design was a large type of bunsen burner.

MAKING STEAM

Very few steam cars used coal burners. Those that did had a system that was self-evident and usually based on railway-engine practice. The vast majority ran on liquid fuel, with a few cars converted to gas.

With liquid fuel the flame could easily be turned on and off, provided some form of relighting was available. The most common method of achieving this was by means of a pilot burner. This was a small flame that not only provided the means for relighting the main part of the burner, but also kept a supply of fuel ready vapourised for use by the burner.

Various ways of supplying the fuel from its tank to the pilot burner were used, normally involving pressurised tanks or mechanical pumps of some kind. Some designs had an entirely separate pilot fuel system, whereas others used the main fuel tank and a separate pump or drew from a small pressurised tank which was in turn fed from the primary tank by the main pump.

Lighting the pilot flame was often difficult. Various methods of pre-heating were used, frequently methylated spirits burnt in a cup device or even a soaked rag, but now many people use a small modern pressurised gas-cylinder torch.

Burner problems were and are one of the weaknesses of the steam car. Dozens of different burner designs were on offer as replacements during its heyday, all claiming to have solved the burner problem, but there was little to choose between them. Most worked on the bunsen burner principle, where the fuel is converted to a gas by pre-heating and is forced into the base of the burner, drawing in air with it to form a vapour, which lights above the burner plate, usually a cast iron or steel plate with a variety of corrugations, slots or holes.

As the steam car developed forced-air type burners were invented, working on the principle of the modern central-heating burner. Most of these were re-inventions of similar designs used for other purposes but proved far more reliable than the bunsen type.

Even when a satisfactory burner had been obtained it still required a supply of correctly pre-heated fuel, delivered at the right pressure at the right time. This entailed a profusion of pumps and valves to try to maintain sufficient fuel for maximum power requirements and yet provide also for total shut-off of the main jets when steam generation was not required, either because working press-ure had been reached, or because the car was stationary. Valves had to be designed to shut off the fuel automatically if the steam pressure was too high and the operator had failed to take any action. In theory this safety device could be left to control the fuel to give a measure of automatic control. In practice persuading it to cut off reliably and cleanly was extremely difficult. If it did not shut smartly, the resultant dribble of fuel still flowing would almost invariably 'light back', that is catch fire outside the burner.

An early experimental steam car, made by Catley and Ayres in 1868. The three-wheel layout was common for pioneer examples of self-powered transport, as it overcame the difficulties that then existed in steering with two wheels. The rear-mounted vertical boiler appears to have no means of stoking the fire once on the move, so when the stored steam had been used the vehicle stopped and then the fire had to be stoked.

EARLY DAYS

The early period can conveniently be considered to run up to and include 1904 and thus correspond with the Veteran Car Club's definition of a veteran car, 1904 being also the latest date for a vehicle that will be accepted by the Royal Automobile Club for its Brighton run.

This period encompasses all the early steam car experiments, such as the Catley and Ayres tricycle of the 1860s, which had a vertical rear-mounted boiler supported on two cart-type wheels, whilst the front of the vehicle rested on a single smaller wheel connected directly to the steering tiller. It seems unlikely that any means of stoking the fire (almost certainly coal) while on the move was provided and thus the range of the car would appear to have been strictly limited.

Various people, in many countries, made single steam vehicles for their own use during the next two decades. The Bollee family from France and the Count De Dion (with his engineers) made a number of such vehicles, some of which were sold to selected members of the public. A few of these could count as cars, as they provided personal transport for two people, but most were more akin to omnibuses, having seats for up to twelve passengers.

The Stanley brothers in the United States can be considered as the fathers of the private steam car, as by far the greatest number of such vehicles were either Stanleys (or the Stanley-designed Locomobiles) or copies of their design.

They started in 1897 and by 1898 had developed the pattern which was to dominate the steam buggy throughout its heyday. This consisted of a relatively lightweight engine, weighing about 50

LEFT: *The 'Craigievar Express' was a crude early one-off design that still exists and has taken part in the Brighton run. In this vehicle it is possible to stoke the fire while on the move, although this is not an easy procedure. The middle mounting of the vertical boiler restricts forward vision, but this is unlikely to be a problem because of the car's low maximum speed.*

BELOW: *This four-wheel Achille Philion dates from 1896. It appears doubtful that the spindly wheels would support the weight of steam equipment for long. It is hardly surprising that early vehicles were the subject of mirth, when such frail devices were produced.*

It is doubtful whether the Lifu (the shortened name of the Liquid Fuel Engineering Company) made any cars itself, but it licensed others to produce its designs between 1899 and 1902. This example supposedly dates from 1896, so it could be a prototype, but it appears to be of idential design, except for the wheelbase, to the 1898-9 3-ton Lifu lorry, also produced in omnibus form.

pounds (23 kg), and a fire-tube boiler. The Stanleys used an unusual boiler design in which the strength of the outer shell was obtained not by thick plate but by a fairly thin skin wound with thousands of yards of piano wire. They devised special machinery to manufacture these boilers, but they provide a major problem for the amateur restorer. The advantage of this method of construction was that the engine weighed only around 100 pounds (45 kg), so, with light running gear and bodywork, a lively little runabout was produced.

This design was so successful that John Walker, the owner of *Cosmopolitan* magazine, persuaded the Stanleys to sell him their car business for 250,000 dollars, about ten times what it had cost them. Walker then produced the car as the Locomobile. Meanwhile the Stanleys redesigned their car to avoid infringing the patents they had sold, in the process making improvements, which they incorporated in the car they offered for sale in 1902. The basic differences were that it had four full elliptic springs in place of the three of the earlier design, and that instead of the engine being vertical in front of the boiler and driving the back axle by chain it was now horizontal and connected directly by spur gears. By the time this design was ready to be sold, Walker had tired of making steamers and sold the Stanley-Locomobile design back to the Stanley brothers for 20,000 dollars. They promptly sold the superseded and unwanted patents to the White company for 15,000 dollars.

The 1902 design continued with minor modifications until the first of the front-boilered cars appeared in 1904. This had a characteristic coffin-nose front, before which there had been little to distinguish the Stanley from any other steam runabout. Very few of these front-boilered cars reached the public before 1905. Previously the unfortunate driver had sat not only on the boiler, but also over a large petrol flame beneath it, so he had to alight quickly when the boiler caught fire externally, as it often did.

ABOVE: *The steam car on the right is an 1887 De Dion three-wheeler, probably the most successful light steam runabout of its time. Several still exist. On the left is a tricycle of 1889 powered by the Count De Dion's most successful invention, a relatively high-speed lightweight petrol engine. In single-cylinder form this engine sold so well during the early twentieth century that the De Dion works gave up making steamers.*

BELOW: *An advertisement for a Locomobile steam car.*

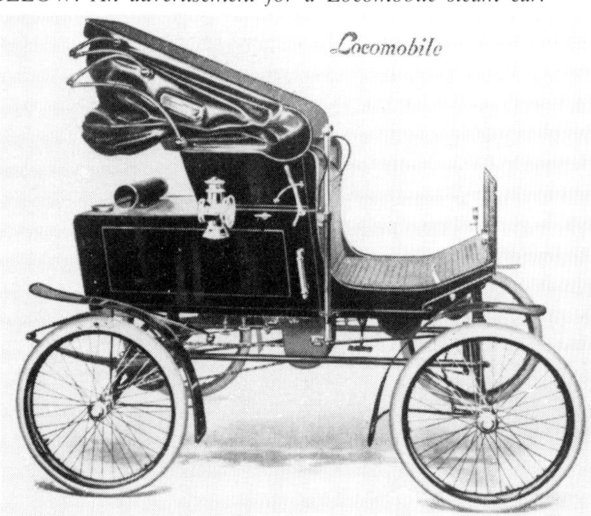

ABOVE: *Little is known about this early steamer, built in the 1890s by M de Bourmont of Arcachon, Gironde, France. It competed in the race from Paris to Rouen on 22nd July 1894, being beaten by all the petrol-engined cars except one. It would seem from the position of the driving sprocket that its engine was under the driver's seat and the boiler at the rear, a similar layout to the early Stanley.*

BELOW: *A Lifu of 1901, with front boiler. The rack-line tubed device at the front is the condenser. The slightly raised bonnet top cover would give access to the top of the boiler. On a heavy vehicle such as this tiller steering would have been hard work.*

ABOVE: *A Gardner-Serpollet of 1903. The design had developed towards a front bonnet by the end of 1903. This housed the water tank and by 1904 the engine had also moved to the front. An enclosed body was not required for this example, which was built for the Maharaja of Rewa and used in India.*

BELOW: *A 1904 model made by the Stanley twins after they recommenced manufacture of steamers. Although they had bought back their patents from Locomobile, they redesigned the buggy to have a horizontal, slightly enlarged engine directly geared to the back axle. The boiler remained vertical and under the driver's seat, which was the rear one.*

A 1901 Serpollet, a car with an early example of a flash boiler, in which steam could be raised quickly to supply a four-cylinder vertical engine, rated at 5 horsepower and fitted with poppet valves. The body was a type often seen around this time. The owner, in this case Lord Northcliffe, travelled in comfort in the rear 'coach', while the chauffeur had to make do with meagre protection in front.

In most early designs steering was by means of a tiller connected to the front wheels, either directly or by a system of levers. With no gearing interposed, road shocks were directly transmitted back to the tiller, and a bump in the road could easily pull the tiller right out of the driver's grasp, if he was either a little weak or not grasping it firmly, which was often difficult with a steamer because there was so much to do with the hands.

Brakes were rudimentary. The Stanley, for example, at first had only a contracting band brake in the centre of the rear axle, acting on the outer of the differential casing, and in practice running in oil, further reducing its retardation effect. Admittedly one could put the engine into reverse, but this was hard on the cylinder heads.

The body was of simple construction, often consisting merely of wooden panels mounted on a wooden frame without even a steel chassis, the whole structure being free to roll on flexible full elliptic springs. This protected the boiler from the worst of the potholes but imparted a peculiar lolloping motion. Sometimes provision was made for four occupants, with a fixed or folding seat either in front of or behind the driver's seat, but usually this was wide enough for only two rather thin people.

In Europe design tended towards more substantial, heavy and expensive cars, but these were made in much smaller numbers than the American buggy. After Bollee and De Dion had given up making steamers, the main European producers were Serpollet and Turner-Meisse. These two makers used the flash boiler.

ABOVE: *This Turner-Meisse of 1904 was fitted with a flash boiler, feeding a three-cylinder single-acting engine rated at 10 horsepower. The condenser at the front, resembling a radiator, could recirculate a large proportion of the water, enabling longer distances to be covered without stopping to refill.*

BELOW: *White was one of the American makes to use a flash boiler, supplying steam to a twin-cylinder compound engine. This car dates from 1905, when White was using a two-speed back axle, and the engine could be disconnected from the axle to run the pumps when the car was stationary. This example was owned by Lord Hothfield, seen with his wife in typical clothes for the period.*

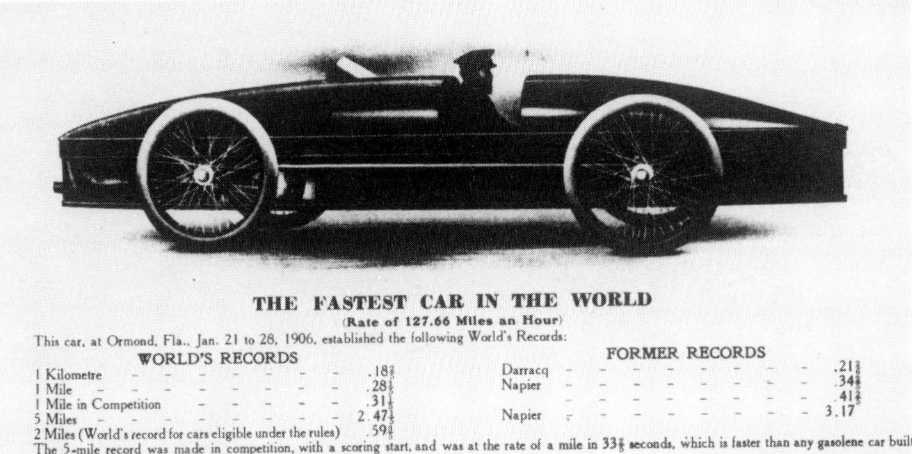

This car, at Ormond, Fla., Jan. 21 to 28, 1906, established the following World's Records:

WORLD'S RECORDS		FORMER RECORDS	
1 Kilometre	.18¾	Darracq	.21½
1 Mile	.28½	Napier	.34⅖
1 Mile in Competition	.31½		.41⅖
5 Miles	2.47½	Napier	3.17
2 Miles (World's record for cars eligible under the rules)	.59⅖		

The 5-mile record was made in competition, with a scoring start, and was at the rate of a mile in 33⅗ seconds, which is faster than any gasolene car built according to A. A. A. rules ever made for a single mile.

The power-plant in this car is exactly like that in the regular Stanley cars, except that it is larger, of about twice the power as the Touring Cars (Model F). It weighs 1,600 pounds, and has margin enough for another boiler of the same size (512 pounds) without passing the racing weight-limit of 2,204 pounds. The boiler is 30 inches in diameter and 18 inches deep. It contains 1,475 tubes, and has a total heating surface of 285 square feet. A steam pressure of 800 to 900 pounds is carried. The engine is 4½ x 6½, and makes 350 revolutions to the mile. The wheels are 34 inches in diameter, and make 600 revolutions to the mile. They are equipped with 3-inch G. and J. tires. The body is so designed that the largest cross-section it presents, including the wheels, is only 9 square feet.

The 1906 Stanley that in January of that year achieved a speed of 127.66 mph (205.44 km/h).

THE DEVELOPING PERIOD, 1905-18

This chapter covers the period from 1905 to 1918, but little development took place during the First World War.

During this time many of the firms that had copied Stanley went out of business, a few more started up with variations on the same theme, and others had their own peculiar ideas, but the general trend was against steam. One of the more unusual shapes was the Grout, which had a round horizontal-shaped boiler bonnet, reminiscent of a steam locomotive, which was advertised as being 'silent and non-explosive'.

Condensers started to become common, and this probably was the greatest improvement of the period, as the necessity to stop for water every 20 miles (32 km) or so had been a great nuisance. The condenser converted the exhaust steam back into water, which could be used again, and this had the added advantage of silencing the car, as well as greatly increasing its range before refilling was required, but even a condensing steamer still lost quite a lot of water.

But in solving one problem another was produced, in this case the difficulty of getting rid of the cylinder lubricating oil that was normally present in the exhaust. Oil on condenser tubes reduces efficiency drastically and inside a boiler it reduces the transfer of heat from the fire to the water, and in extreme cases can result in a tube burning through.

Various types of oil or grease separator were tried, different designs being favoured by various companies, but the purpose was always the same, to remove as much oil and grease from the exhaust as early as possible. Many worked on the principle of centrifugal force, the steam

ABOVE: *Two Whites of about 1906. Note the twisted mudguards and well used appearance. The nicked tyre treads were common in the early days. The lack of headlights was not uncommon: the cars would not have been used at night, and lamps were an additional expense.*

BELOW: *A Serpollet racer, with Leon Serpollet at the wheel. An early attempt at streamlining, this vehicle was nicknamed the 'Easter Egg' and rated at 16 horsepower. It was built for sprints and may not have competed with its burner alight, having raised steam beforehand. The wingnuts against the inner edge of the wheel rims locate T-shape bolts that protrude into the centre of the tyre beads in order to stop them coming off the wheels.*

LEFT: *This condenser, at the front of a 1904 Turner-Meisse, looks like the petrol car radiators of the period. The series of gilled or finned tubes takes the exhaust steam, cools it and returns it to the water supply tank as water. The main problem was first to remove the cylinder lubricating oil.*

BELOW: *One of the chores of steam car operation was sucking up water from a stream to refill the water tank. A special steam-powered suction device was provided for this purpose on all later Stanleys. The operator had to filter the water carefully or valves and pump plungers would soon need attention. Making sure a water supply was available every 20 miles (32 km) or so was one of the essentials of operating a non-condensing steamer.*

being swirled around and the oil flung out so that it could be drained off.

The Gardner-Serpollet had ceased production by 1907 and Turner-Meisse had stopped making steam cars by 1913, by which time the best known American maker using a flash boiler, White, had also given up steamers, after just over ten years, in favour of petrol cars.

The White design for a steam car was heavier than the Stanley buggy type and much more expensive, catering for wealthier customers, one of whom was President Taft. The flash type of boiler required the application of exactly the right amount of heat relative to the steam needs, and the correct amount of water had to be pumped in, for the White did not have the tolerance of those cars with fire-tube boilers. With a flash boiler, if the tube became empty with the fire full on, a section of tube very quickly burned through, and it was difficult to repair.

A typical White engine looked from the outside quite similar to a petrol car engine, inasmuch as it was vertical at the front under a bonnet, with vertical valves and a conventional crankshaft, from which the drive was taken via a shaft to a normal back axle. There were detail variations between years and models, but the principle varied very little.

Another American vehicle introduced and later discontinued during this period was the Ross. This too had a front-mounted vertical engine, having two cylinders rated at 25 horsepower and using Stephenson valve gear. The boiler supplied steam at a working pressure of 375 pounds per square inch (26 kg/sq cm) and was claimed to give an easy 35 to 45 miles per hour (56 to 72 km/h). Prices were quoted between 2250 and 2800 dollars.

The Lane survived longer, from 1901 to 1909. Originally a typical steam buggy, by 1905 it had developed into a bigger, more powerful vehicle with a two cylinder compound engine rated at 15 horsepower, and fitted with a condenser. It was claimed to cover between 7 and 10 miles per gallon (2.5 to 3.5 km/litre) of fuel. The last of the line had an engine rated at 30 horsepower, with a semi-flash boiler, and cost 3,100 dollars.

The Morriss dated from 1908 and had a production run of about three years, being designed by Frank Morriss. It had a two-cylinder engine with slide valves, of his own design, and was usually fitted with a four-seater body of the type shown. This was one of the very few British steamers.

The life of the Doble company is usually said to run from 1914 to 1931 but Doble produced this steam-powered buckboard in 1912. A primitive experiment, it bore little relation to the very sophisticated steam cars that this maker started to produce in the 1920s.

BETWEEN THE WARS

The period from the end of the First World War until the start of the Second saw the demise of the steam car as a commercial proposition. This was due not solely to the improvements that had taken place in the petrol car, but also in part to the fact that cars had ceased to be amusing toys to all but a very few eccentrics. To the majority they had become a serious and often essential means of transport, and so there was little room for any difference from the norm, whether it was a variation on the petrol car design or a steamer.

The two best known steam cars of this era of decline were the Stanley and a newcomer, the very complex and sophisticated Doble.

The Stanley was basically an updated version of the previous design, being a little more complicated and having a better burner. Externally it was made to look more like a petrol car, having its condenser in the shape of a radiator and the boiler hidden under a conventional bonnet. An electric supply was provided to run the lights, with a battery charged by a generator driven by the back axle.

The Doble was an entirely different concept. Abner Doble was a very clever engineer, who knew that a successful steam car had to be capable of being operated as easily as the current internal combustion engined cars. Thus he endeavoured to make the feeds to boiler and burner fully automatic, and it was this complication that not only made the Doble much more expensive than most ordinary cars but also frightened the public. Local garages almost always warned against buying such a device, and anyone who did had to be prepared to learn how to look after it himself, as professional help was most difficult to obtain. It is doubtful if Abner Doble even wished to sell a great quantity. Many of the comparatively few private car examples of the marque were based on the chassis and running gear of contemporary petrol cars. A few steam buses were also made, mostly for export rather than for use in the maker's own country, the United States.

All these machines were well made and used a variety of engine designs, mainly of either twin-cylinder or four-cylinder double-acting compound layout, with a ratio of low to high pressure cylinder

A 1921 Stanley. This firm was probably the most prolific of all steam car makers. By this date it was difficult to tell a steamer from a petrol car by the exterior. This is a typical square-rigged two-door coupé of the American style of this period, with the condenser closely resembling a radiator.

diameters of about two to one, using the same stroke for all cylinders connected to a common crankshaft. Normally these cylinders were cast in pairs with integral valve chests to each block. Extensive use of roller and ball bearings was made throughout. In some cases the engine crankcase was cast integral with the rear-axle centre casing. In others a separate engine crankcase was bolted either direct or via an adaptor plate to the rear-axle casing of a proprietary petrol car, usually an expensive type like a Lincoln. In both cases the drive was by means of a spur gear on the crankshaft meshing with another spur gear surrounding the differential.

The valve gear was either slide or piston type, in which it was not uncommon for one valve to be made to function for both one high and one low pressure cylinder. These were operated by the Stephenson link motion, giving provision for various cut-off points, apart from a reverse position. Usually three positions were provided, operated by a pedal with notches to hold it in each position. A Doble in good condition would run happily at 50 to 60 mph (80 to 97 km/h) on hook-up. To engage reverse a catch was lifted and this pedal pushed right down.

The boiler, or, as they preferred to call it, the steam generator, was seamless steel tubing, about 600 feet (183 m) long, coiled into an assembly around 2 feet (0.6 m) square by 1 foot (0.3 m) high, and tested to around 7000 pounds per square inch (492 kg/sq cm) cold water pressure. This coil was contained in a double-wall case, having an inner lining of nickel-chrome steel with an outer casing of aluminium, the space between the two being filled with an efficient insulator, often silocel.

To this casing was bolted the combustion chamber, again with inner and outer walls enclosing insulation. The mixture of fuel and air was forced into this chamber for combustion, by means of a blower

24

fan. This was one of the advanced features of the Doble, also used by other makes as the steamer developed. Forcing the mixture into the combustion chamber largely eliminated the old problem of burner blow-back.

The pressure for force-feeding this mixture was obtained, in the case of the Doble, by electric power, an electric motor driving what was in effect a fan. Fuel supply was governed by a float chamber and control was by switching on or off, no half-speed refinement proving necessary. When steam pressure was high enough the blower switched off, and it came on again when needed. To make this work satisfactorily ignition was by means of an electric spark plug; thus the whole burner assembly was a great advance on the simple bunsen type used by early steamers.

The correct amount of water feed had to be synchronised and supplied automatically to the boiler tube. To achieve this, an auxiliary unit was driven by a shaft from the main engine and contained the pumps for fuel, water, vacuum and oiling systems, and in addition the electric generator, which when the car was stationary could double as a motor to drive the unit to provide fuel and water feeds if needed. When used thus, the main drive was disconnected.

There were several water pumps which were switched in and out as needed, by a system of electric controls regulated by the temperature and pressure of the steam. All were needed at once only when maximum power was required. This control system was by far the most complex part of the car.

The used steam was condensed in what looked like a normal radiator, after first passing through an oil separator. The condenser was cooled by a large fan also driven from the auxiliary unit.

Another marque produced in the 1920s was the Delling. This vehicle had both the square-shaped boiler and the vertical three-cylinder engine situated at the front under a bonnet of conventional shape, with the by now usual radiator-shaped condenser. The engine was claimed to produce over 60 horsepower, giving a speed of at least 60 mph (97 km/h). Unlike in a petrol car, this horsepower could, if needed, be available at zero engine speed, and so acceleration was good. In 1925 this car had Lockheed hydraulic brakes on all four wheels, a very early application not only of four-wheel brakes but also of a hydraulic system.

The chassis was the usual pressed steel of the period. The engine was connected directly to the rear axle by means of a shaft. Two body styles were offered, a sedan and a four-seater roadster or phaeton, priced between 2500 and 3500 dollars, compared to the Doble at around

An American steam car, a quaint four-door body on a chassis made in the 1920s by Thomas Derr, a well known steam car engineer and improver. Apart from special steam parts, generally of Stanley type, the mechanical basis of the car was the Hudson, which in petrol-engined form was one of the fastest saloons of its day.

A Doble model E sedan of 1924. Abner Doble aimed to make the controls as easy as those of the petrol car, with most operations automatic. To achieve this, a complex system of mechanical devices was required to regulate fuel and water supplies.

8000 dollars and the last of the Stanleys, about 1927, around 2500 dollars.

Virtually all the main steam car manufacturers had given up production by 1930. From then until the Second World War most steamers were private conversions of existing petrol cars, mostly in the United States, and many using an old Stanley power unit. These engines seldom wore out and so many were saved when the rest of the car was scrapped, to become readily available to these 'special' builders. They are still advertised from time to time, as are the Locomobile type. Being a compact entity, this engine could be grafted conveniently into almost any conventional rear axle, either by direct gearing, or by chain or spur gears into the existing transmission.

This beautiful drophead coupé, a series E Doble of 1925, has lines to match those of any petrol car. The engine was a four-cylinder double-acting compound type providing around 120 horsepower.

This car was made by Charles Keen long after the Second World War, incorporating developments he had devised over the years. It has a purpose-built modern sports-car body. In 1968 the car was one of the vehicles examined by the Senate Commerce Committee in the USA as part of their anti-smog investigations.

STEAM CARS SINCE 1940

During the Second World War a few steam cars appeared on the roads, and because of the scarcity of private cars in use these steamers received far more publicity than their numbers justified. The reason for their appearance was that petrol was either rationed or not available at all but it was still sometimes possible to obtain a fuel that would run a steam car. Nearly all these vehicles were old steam cars, but a few consisted of an old engine put into a relatively modern car.

Since 1945 only a very few steam cars have been produced. What steam work has been done has consisted mainly of experiments by major car manufacturers, particularly in the United States, seeking to find an alternative to the petrol engine to overcome the problem of noxious emissions.

The Californian state assembly set up its own project to develop a 'clean' vehicle and initially experimented with steam buses. These ran about 10,000 miles (16,000 km), partly with fare-paying passengers, before attention was turned to private cars. They tried a steam turbine mounted in a 1973 Chevrolet Vega coupé, and a four-cylinder compound expansion piston engine fitted to a

Ford Pinto. The performance standards aimed at were a speed of 70 mph (113 km/h) on the level, 50 mph (80 km/h) up a 5 per cent gradient, and the ability to drive off within thirty seconds from cold, and achieve maximum power within three minutes.

Information on the experiments in steam by the major car companies is scarce as they seldom divulged details of their work. However, General Motors admitted to at least two designs, the SE-101 and the SE-124. The more successful seems to have been the SE-101. This had a four-cylinder single-acting engine with overhead inlet valves and exhausted via ports in the cylinder wall at the bottom of the stroke. The total capacity was 101 cubic inches (1655 cc). It drove the rear axle via a continuously variable toric transmission, allowing the engine to idle when the car was at rest, to drive the various accessories by means of belts and electric clutches, all monitored by over twenty relays and sensors. The boiler was of water-tube type with series-parallel flow, heated by two 10 inch (254 mm) burners based on gas-turbine design, and fed by a fuel pump synchronised with an air blower. The condenser needed two 20 inch (508 mm) fans for cooling, which absorbed about 22 horse-power. These together with other accessories consumed so much power that the car had to struggle to reach 50 mph (80 km/h) in 30 seconds. Fuel consumption was very great, at around 4 miles per gallon (1 km/litre).

Ford tried a conversion in one of their big Fairlane sedans, using steam plant made by the Williams Engine Company, but this was abandoned when it proved uneconomic. Several other small companies made experimental steam vehicles: Smith and Petreson converted a Volkswagen, and Robert McCulloch produced the Paxton Phoenix, for which Abner Doble designed the engine, applying the benefits of technology invented since his own company's last production, but again costs and the highly complicated control gear killed it.

In Britain Singer, Donald Healey and Alex Moulton tried their hands at steam cars after the war, and all turned to more profitable work. Thomas Hindle, an expert on the early Serpollet cars, spent much time designing modern steam engines, but none of these went into serious production.

However, as the external combustion engine of the steamer is by nature far less efficient than the internal combustion type used in the ordinary petrol car, when the fuel crisis came in the 1970s steam development was largely abandoned. Most of the previous research had been devoted to finding an alternative and more efficient type of engine, even turbines having been considered. The basic theory behind these efforts was that to obtain the best use of energy steam should enter the engine as hot as possible and exhaust as cold as possible.

One of the engine characteristics that was tried in various forms was the uniflow, in which steam enters at the ends and exhausts in the middle. The object was to produce a uniform direction of steam and thus a uniform temperature gradient in the engine to minimise losses caused by continually heating and cooling the valves and occurring if the same valve is used for admission and exit of steam. As in the early years, different types of valve and valve-operating gear were championed by different people, but no type appeared to have any clear advantage over the others.

Charles Keen converted a 1948 Plymouth tourer by mounting a V4 steam engine at the rear, with a front boiler consuming water at the average rate of 25 miles per gallon (9 km/litre), and fuel at 16 miles per gallon (6 km/litre). In the late 1950s Keen mounted another of his designs in a fibreglass sports body made

In the 1960s and early 1970s most of the major American car manufacturers experimented with steam cars to see if modern technology made them more viable than in the past. This example by General Motors, type SE-101, dates from about 1968-9.

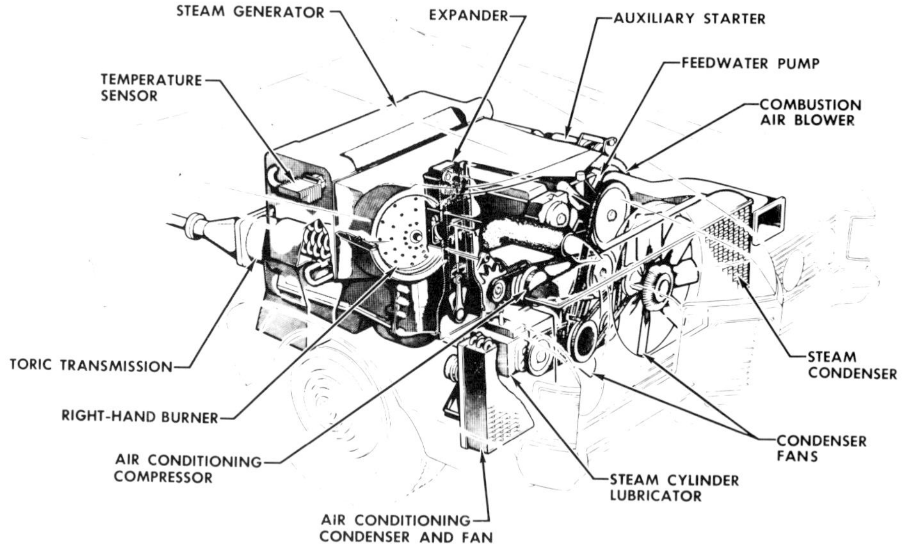

The Besler power plant in the GM SE-124 steam car. The large cylindrical object is the combustion chamber and steam generator, with the combustion air blower attached to its side. The feedwater tank is mounted on the fire wall.

by Victress but subsequently sold his interests to the Thermal Kinetics Company of New York.

Bill Lear experimented with various types of steam application to vehicles, mostly turbines. Many were fitted to buses, but he converted a racing car and put one of his bus engines into a Chevrolet Monte Carlo sedan. However, having spent around 4 million dollars, with no apparent sign that the vehicles could ever be sold at a high enough price to cover their cost, Lear decided not to pursue his developments to a commercial stage.

Today there are two main reasons why the steamer will not in the foreseeable future become commonplace as a private car. The first is the oldest problem of all, heating the water to make enough steam at the right time; the second is modern industry and economics. The only way to make a product cheap enough for the masses is to make it in mass: if it cannot be produced in tens of thousands, then it cannot be produced cheaply enough to gain a large market. After several years of research into steam cars, General Motors concluded that their advantages were far outweighed by their disadvantages, which included poor fuel economy, low power output in relation to the size of the power unit, unreliability and difficulty in servicing.

RUNNING A STEAM CAR

It is essential that a steam car is insured for boiler and other risks to third parties.

A steam car needs steam, for which water is necessary. Thus, first of all, the tanks for water, fuel and oil must be filled. The water must be soft; anyone who has seen the inside of a kettle used with hard water will know why. If petrol is the fuel, it must be non-leaded, obtained by special order from a fuel wholesaler at three times the normal price. Oil must be special steam type.

Even when the water tank is full, the boiler may well be empty if it was not siphoned full after the car's last use. The water must then be laboriously pumped

General Motors researchers install the combustion system and steam generator in the experimental vehicle GM SE-101, a modified 1969 Pontiac Grand Prix. Already mounted in the engine compartment is the 160 horsepower four-cylinder expander. The SE-101 was developed by General Motors to permit evaluation of the vapour cycle engine under operating conditions.

in by hand or a garden hose could be connected to the blow-down valve to bring the level up. Flash boilers do not have this problem, as a few hand pumps will fill the tube.

If there is a pressure-fed burner there is no more hard work to do, especially if the car also has electric ignition. If, however, the vehicle has a Stanley-type natural draught burner, as is more common, then lighting up the engine is likely to be extremely troublesome.

The first step is to work up the pressure on the pilot fuel and then apply a blowlamp to the pilot vapouriser, the associated pipework and fittings, both inside and outside the burner casing. There is a peep-hole, which should be large enough to take the nozzle of the blowlamp. (If it is not, enlarge it.) When all is reasonably hot, and this may take ten to fifteen minutes, keep the blowlamp

in this orifice and turn on the pilot fuel valve. With luck the pipework will be hot enough to produce a jet of fully vapourised fuel that will light above the burner plate as required. More likely, if the jet has not been 'pricked' clear, nothing will come out, or alternatively a jet of wet fuel will run out, some into the lower half of the burner, some on to the floor. At this point the natural reaction is to panic, pull the blowlamp out, and set the whole thing on fire. Normally this will go out on its own without destroying the car or doing any damage, but a fire extinguisher should always be kept close to hand, in case it does not.

Having shut off the fuel valve and disposed of the spilt fuel and the blocked jet, try again. Once the pilot light has lighted satisfactorily, leave the blowlamp in place adding heat for a few minutes, then turn it off and withdraw, shutting the peep-hole, letting the pilot run long enough to get the main vapouriser coil and the burner casing warm to hot. This may take fifteen minutes or more. During this time the main jets must be 'pricked' clear and, if the main fuel supply is separate from the pilot fuel, then the pressure of this feed must be brought up by hand, and the air balance tank, if any, primed.

Turn on the engine cylinder oil feed and go round all the engine and chassis joints with an oil gun, including the cross-head slides and eccentrics. Make sure the cylinder drain cock is open and both throttle and back-up valve are shut.

It is now necessary to guess the state of the main vapouriser and whether it is hot enough to allow the main fuel valve to be opened. If you think it is, try opening this valve. The choices are the same as for the pilot light, except that if you are wrong there will be a bigger puddle of fuel on the floor and a bigger fire. The pilot light usually goes out at this stage and if you try to relight it there will be a big but not destructive bang, as the unburnt fuel forms an explosive mixture with the air in the burner. This often singes your eyebrows and causes you to jump back, invariably hitting yourself on some sharp object behind you.

When finally the main burner functions properly, it should raise steam to working pressure and cut off automatically.

The car is now almost ready to move off, but first steam must be allowed to dribble through the cylinders to warm them. Otherwise it is likely to go only a few yards before hydraulically wrecking the engine. In theory the main burner will start again as the steam pressure drops. However, after a mile or so, it may happen that the burner has lighted back outside its casing and fuel is flaming all round you. Quickly shut all the valves and wait for the fire to go out. If the valve on the mechanical water pump is not closed the boiler will be nearly emptied and it will take half an hour to refill it by laboriously hand-pumping water. The pilot light, however, must not be shut off when the main fuel valve is being closed, or the entire lighting-up procedure will have to be gone through again by the roadside.

Steam cars are unpredictable. After giving so much trouble that the owner determines to get rid of his machine, it suddenly starts to behave perfectly. Then all he has to do as he drives along is watch the pressures of steam, main and pilot fuels, control the valves for these fluids, check the oil feed, keep an eye on the water level and feed water to the boiler, and occasionally steer, when a hand can be spared from operating the pumps.

FURTHER READING

Bentley, John. *Old Time Steam Cars*, Fawcett Books, Connecticut, USA.

Bird, Anthony. *The Steam Car.* 1975.

Derr, Thomas. *The Modern Steam Car.* Floyd Clymer, Los Angeles, USA.

Evans, Richard J. *Restoring and Collecting Steam Engines.* TAB Books, Blue Ridge Summit, Pennsylvania, USA, 1980.

Stein, Ralph. *The Stanley Steamer.*

Woodbury, George. *The Story of the Stanley Steamer.* Floyd Clymer, Los Angeles, USA, 1967.

Proceedings of the Institute of Automotive Engineers, 24th August 1970. Institute of Automotive Engineers, New York, NY 10001, USA.

The Steam Automobile (monthly magazine), Hunt Road, Pleasant Garden, North Carolina, USA.

Steam Car Scrapbook. Floyd Clymer, Los Angeles, USA.

PLACES TO VISIT

Intending visitors are advised to find out the times of opening before making a special journey to a museum.

GREAT BRITAIN

British Commercial Vehicle Museum, King Street, Leyland, Preston, Lancashire PR5 1LE. Telephone: Preston (0772) 451011.

Hull Transport and Archaeology Museum, 36 High Street, Hull, North Humberside. Telephone: Hull (0482) 222737.

Manx Motor Museum, Crosby, Isle of Man. Telephone: Marown (0624) 851236.

National Motor Museum, John Montagu Building, Beaulieu, Brockenhurst, Hampshire SO4 7ZN. Telephone: Beaulieu (0590) 612345.

Shuttleworth Collection of Historic Aeroplanes, Cars and Bicycles, Old Warden Aerodrome, Biggleswade, Bedfordshire. Telephone: Northill (076 727) 288.

AUSTRALIA AND NEW ZEALAND

Birdwood Mill Pioneer Art and Historical Motor Museum, Shannon Street, Birdwood, South Australia 5234.

Heytesbury Collection, George Street, Perth, Western Australia.

Science Museum of Victoria, 304-328 Swanston Street, Melbourne, Victoria 3000, Australia.

Southward Museum, Lower Hutt, Wellington, New Zealand.

Vintage and Veteran Car Museum, Coolangatta, Gold Coast, Queensland 4225, Australia.

Yaldhurst Transport Museum, Christchurch, Canterbury Province, New Zealand.

EUROPE

Aalholm Motor Museum, Schloss Aalholm, Nysted, Denmark.

Carlo Biscaretti di Ruffia Motor Museum, Corso Unità d'Italia 40, Turin, Italy.

Deutsches Museum, Museum Insel, 8000 Munich, Bavaria, West Germany.

Eppstein Motor Museum, Hauptstrasse, Eppstein, Hessen, West Germany.

French Motor Museum, Château de Rochetaillé, 69001 Lyons, France.

Institute of Technology, Oslo, Norway.

Lips Autoron, Grotestraat 63, 5150 AB Drunen, Noord Brabant, Holland.

Lourdes Motor Museum, Lourdes, France.

Museum of Industry and Technology, Mariahilferstrasse 212, 1140 Vienna 14, Austria.

National Museum of Road Transport and Tourism, Palais de Compiègne, 60200 Compiègne, Oise, France.

Provincial Automobile Museum, Domein Kelchterhoef 3530, Houthalen, Limburg, Belgium.

Quattoroute, Via Achille Grandi, Milan, Italy.

UNITED STATES OF AMERICA

Bellm's Cars of Yesteryear, North Tamiami Trail, Sarasota, Florida.

Frederick C. Crawford Auto-Aviation Museum of the Western Reserve Historical Society, 10825 East Boulevard, Cleveland, Ohio 44106.

Greenfield Village and Henry Ford Museum, Oakwood Boulevard, Dearborn, Michigan 48121.

Harrah's Automobile Collection, PO Box 10, Reno, Nevada 89504.

Heritage Plantation of Sandwich, Grove Street, Sandwich, Massachusetts 02563.

Marshall Collection, Yorklyn, Delaware.

Smithsonian Institution, 1000 Jefferson Drive SW, Washington, DC 20560.

Veteran Car Museum, 2030 South Cherokee, Denver, Colorado 80223.